AF598704
CELTICS
0
BOSTON CELTICS
ALL-TIME GREATS
BY BRENDAN FLYNN
CELTICS
33

Book design by Jake Slavik
Cover design by Jake Slavik

Photographs ©: Winslow Townson/AP Images, cover (top), 1 (top); Dave Tenenbaum/AP Images, cover (bottom), 1 (top); Robert Kingsbury/Sporting News/Getty Images, 4; Fred Kaplan /Sports Illustrated/Getty Images, 6; Focus on Sport/Getty Images, 7, 13, 14, 17; Jonathan Kirn/Getty Images Sport/Getty Images, 8; Matt Campbell/AFP/Getty Images, 9; Bettmann/Getty Images, 10; Steve Lipofsky/Sports Illustrated/Getty Images, 18; Winslow Townson/Sports Illustrated/Getty Images, 20; Red Line Editorial, 22

Press Box Books, an imprint of Press Room Editions.

ISBN
978-1-63494-150-1 (library bound)
978-1-63494-163-1 (paperback)
978-1-63494-176-1 (epub)
978-1-63494-189-1 (hosted ebook)

Library of Congress Control Number: 2019951047

Distributed by North Star Editions, Inc.
2297 Waters Drive
Mendota Heights, MN 55120
www.northstareditions.com

Printed in the United States of America
012020

ABOUT THE AUTHOR

Brendan Flynn is a San Francisco resident and an author of numerous children's books. In addition to writing about sports, Flynn also enjoys competing in triathlons, Scrabble tournaments, and chili cook-offs.

TABLE OF CONTENTS

SHARMAN
21
BOSTO

CHAPTER 1

SHARPSHOOTERS

The Boston Celtics are one of the NBA's best teams. They began play in 1946–47 before the league was called the NBA. The Celtics had won 17 NBA titles through the 2018–19 season. That's more than any other team.

The Celtics have had many great players along the way. Some of them were known as excellent shooters. One of their first stars was **Bill Sharman**. He played for Boston from 1951 to 1961. Sharman's dead-eye shooting helped drive the Celtics' offense. He led the league in free-throw percentage seven times too.

In 1957 another great shooter arrived in Boston. **Sam Jones** was an expert at the bank shot. He used it from either side of the hoop to score a lot of points.

RULE CHANGES

In 1954 the NBA added a 24-second shot clock to speed up the game. The three-point line was introduced in 1979. Both rule changes made good shooters even more valuable.

Jones was a clutch player. He often saved his best work for the playoffs. He won 10 NBA titles in 12 years in Boston.

Jo Jo White was a star guard throughout the 1970s. White was great at shooting off the dribble. He was a strong passer too. And he was durable. White played in 488 games in a row. That's a team record.

Larry Bird arrived in Boston in 1979. Bird was an outstanding all-around player. He could pass, rebound, and score as well as anyone in the league. He averaged 24.3 points per game during his 13-year career. Bird was deadly from three-point land. He won the NBA Three-Point Shootout three times. He also led the Celtics to three NBA titles.

Paul Pierce joined the team in 1998. He soon became one of the league's best players. A 10-time All-Star, he averaged 23.7 points per game over a nine-year span. He used his size and skills to create space for his shot all over the court.

STAT SPOTLIGHT

MOST CAREER THREE-POINTERS

CELTICS TEAM RECORD

Paul Pierce: 1,823

COUSY
14

CHAPTER 2

PLAYMAKERS

Good shooters need strong passers to get them the ball. The Celtics had one of the best passers in the game in **Bob Cousy**. He's considered the first great NBA point guard. Cousy's nickname was "the Houdini of the Hardwood." That's because he was a magician on the court. Cousy could dribble out of any jam. And he always seemed to find a teammate open for a shot.

Cousy joined the Celtics in 1950–51. He spent 13 seasons in Boston. He was an All-Star in each of them. Cousy led the NBA in assists eight years in a row.

For 16 seasons, **John Havlicek** did a little bit of everything for the Celtics. His hustle and smarts made him a threat all over the court. He could shoot. He could pass. He could rebound. Havlicek's most famous play was on defense.

The Philadelphia 76ers were in Boston for Game 7 of the 1965 Eastern Conference Finals. In the final seconds, the 76ers had a chance to win the game. But Havlicek stole the inbounds pass. He passed it to Sam Jones, who dribbled out the clock. The Celtics went on to win the NBA title.

FAMOUS CALL

"Havlicek stole the ball!" It's one of the most famous radio calls in sports history. Longtime Celtics radio announcer Johnny Most made it. He's still remembered for his description of Havlicek's big play against the 76ers.

STAT SPOTLIGHT

MOST CAREER GAMES

CELTICS TEAM RECORD

John Havlicek: 1,270

RUSSELL
6
13
PHILA
76
CELTICS
6
3
PH

CHAPTER 3
BIG MEN

Over the years, Boston has been home to some of the NBA's top centers and power forwards. None had more impact than **Bill Russell**. He came to Boston as a rookie in 1956. Russell specialized in rebounding. He averaged 22.5 rebounds per game over his 13-year career. He led the league five times, including a career-high 24.7 in 1963–64.

Russell was an outstanding shot blocker. He had a famous rivalry with Wilt Chamberlain, another legendary center. Chamberlain usually put up better statistics, but Russell usually came away with the victory.

Russell also served as a player-coach during his final three seasons in Boston. He was the first black head coach in NBA history. In those three seasons, Russell led the Celtics to the final two championships of their epic dynasty.

THE DYNASTY

The Celtics' run from 1956–57 to 1968–69 is considered the NBA's longest dynasty. In those 13 seasons, Boston won 11 NBA titles. The great **Red Auerbach** was the Celtics' head coach for the first nine of them. Russell was on the court for all 11 championships.

Boston found another great big man a year after Russell retired. **Dave Cowens** was a double-double machine throughout the 1970s. At just 6'9" he was smaller than most other centers. But he made up for it with hard work and determination. Cowens averaged 17.6 points and 13.6 rebounds per game over his career.

COWENS
18

McHALE
32

PARISH
00

STAT SPOTLIGHT

CAREER BLOCKS PER GAME

CELTICS TEAM RECORD

Kevin McHale: 1.7

The Celtics won three NBA titles in the 1980s. **Robert Parish** and **Kevin McHale** played a huge role. Parish took over at center for Cowens. He was a steady presence near the hoop. Parish was a strong defender and rebounder. He was known for high-arcing jump shots that splashed through the hoop.

McHale spent most of his first five seasons coming off the bench. He worked endlessly on his footwork near the basket. The moves he developed made him a dangerous scorer down low. His turnaround fadeaway jumper was impossible to defend along the baseline.

In 2007 the Celtics traded for veteran forward **Kevin Garnett**. He had just led the NBA in rebounding four straight seasons with Minnesota. In his first year with the Celtics, Garnett led the team to the NBA title.

TATUM
0
CELTICS
0

CHAPTER 4
MODERN STARS

Boston won its last NBA title in 2007–08. But the Celtics have been building a team that can get back to the NBA Finals. **Jayson Tatum** joined the Celtics in 2017. The smooth-shooting forward averaged almost 15 points per game over his first two seasons.

Point guard **Kemba Walker** joined the Celtics as a free agent before the 2019–20 season. Walker spent his first eight NBA seasons in Charlotte, making the All-Star team in his last three years with the Hornets. In 2018–19 he averaged 25.6 points per game, a career-best total.

TIMELINE

1946
1950
BILL SHARMAN
(1951-52 TO 1960-61)
BOB COUSY
(1950-51 TO 1962-63)
1960
SAM JONES
(1957-58 TO 1968-69)
BILL RUSSELL
(1956-57 TO 1968-69)
JOHN HAVLICEK
(1962-63 TO 1977-78)
1970
JO JO WHITE
(1969-70 TO 1978-79)
DAVE COWENS
(1970-71 TO 1979-80)
1980
LARRY BIRD
(1979-80 TO 1991-92)
KEVIN McHALE
(1980-81 TO 1992-93)
ROBERT PARISH
(1980-81 TO 1993-94)
1990
2000
PAUL PIERCE
(1998-99 TO 2012-13)
KEVIN GARNETT
(2007-08 TO 2012-13)
2010
JAYSON TATUM
(2017-18 TO PRESENT)
KEMBA WALKER
(2019-20 TO PRESENT)
2020

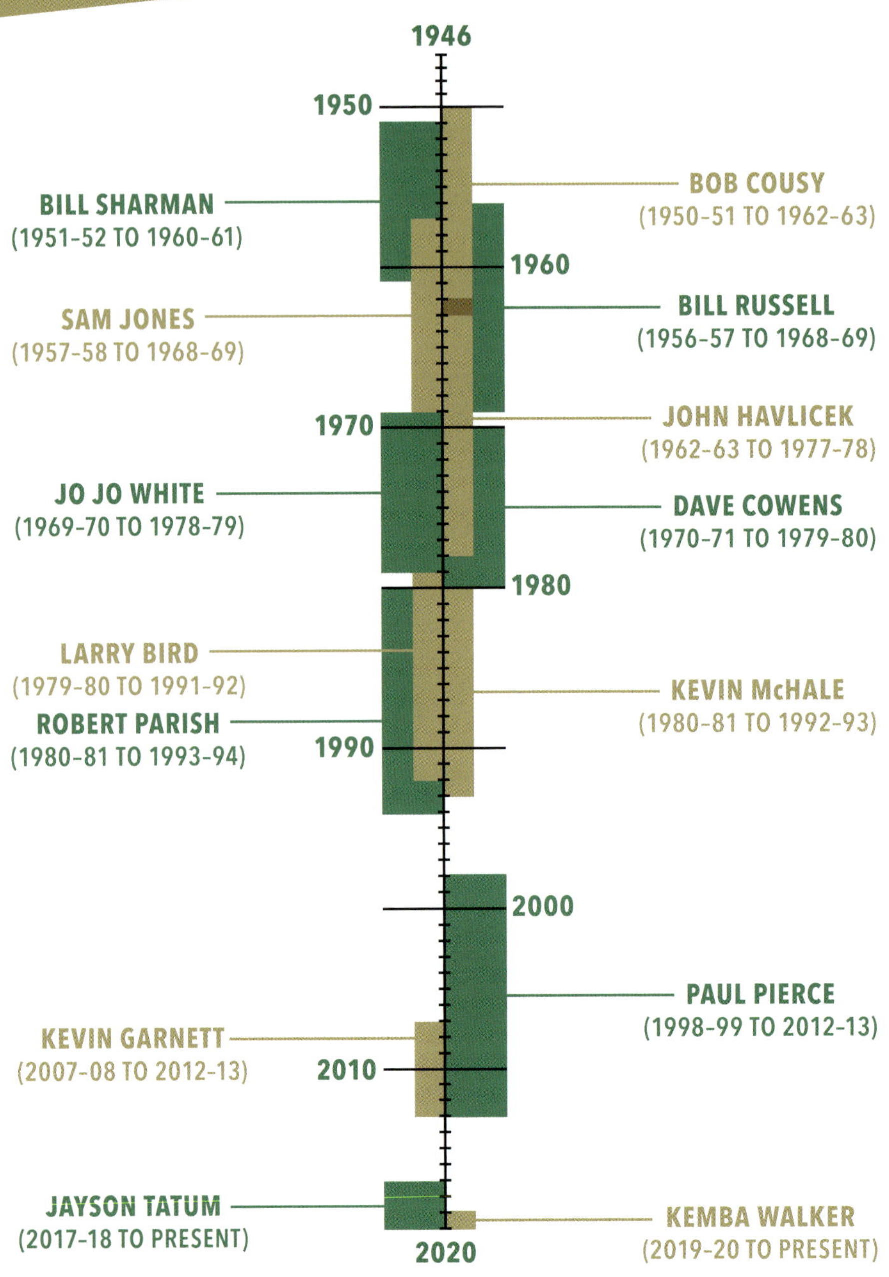

TEAM FACTS

BOSTON CELTICS

First season: 1946–47

NBA championships: 17*

Key coaches:

Red Auerbach (1950–51 to 1965–66)

795–397, 90–58 playoffs, 9 NBA titles

Tom Heinsohn (1969–70 to 1977–78)

427–263, 47–33 playoffs, 2 NBA titles

K. C. Jones (1983–84 to 1987–88)

308–102, 65–37 playoffs, 2 NBA titles

Doc Rivers (2004–05 to 2012–13)

416–305, 59–47 playoffs, 1 NBA title

MORE INFORMATION

To learn more about the Boston Celtics, go to **pressboxbooks.com/AllAccess**.

These links are routinely monitored and updated to provide the most current information available.

**Through 2018–19 season*

GLOSSARY

bank shot
A shot that is designed to bounce off the backboard before going into the hoop.

clutch
Able to come through in important or pressure-packed situations.

double-double
Accumulating 10 or more of two certain statistics in a game.

durable
Tough, long-lasting.

dynasty
A team that has an extended period of success, usually winning multiple championships in the process.

fadeaway
A shot taken while moving away from the basket.

rivalry
A fierce, ongoing competition with an opponent.

shot clock
A clock that counts down the number of seconds remaining before a basketball team must shoot the ball.

turnaround
A shot that begins with the shooter's back to the basket.

INDEX